J 973.313 HAR
Harris, Nancy, 1956-
What's the Declaration of
Independence? /

D1226383

PALM BEACH COUNTY
LIBRARY SYSTEM
3650 SUMMIT BLVD.
WEST PALM BEACH, FLORIDA 33406

First Guide to Government

What's the Declaration of Independence?

Nancy Harris

Heinemann Library
Chicago, IL

HEINEMANN-RAINTREE

TO ORDER:

☎ Phone Customer Service **888-454-2279**

💻 Visit **www.heinemannraintree.com** to browse our catalog and order online.

©2008 Heinemann-Raintree
a division of Pearson Education Limited
Chicago, Illinois

All rights reserved. No part of this publication may be reproduced or transmitted in any form or by any means, electronic or mechanical, including photocopying, recording, taping, or any information storage and retrieval system, without permission in writing from the publisher.

Editorial: Rebecca Rissman
Design: Kimberly R. Miracle and Betsy Wernert
Illustrations: Mapping Specialists
Photo Research: Tracy Cummins and Heather Mauldin
Production: Duncan Gilbert

Originated by Modern Age
Printed in China by South China Printing Company
The paper used to print this book comes from sustainable resources.

ISBN-13: 978-1-4329-0984-0 (hc)
ISBN-10: 1-4329-0984-3 (hc)
ISBN-13: 978-1-4329-0990-1 (pb)
ISBN-10: 1-4329-0990-8 (pb)

10 09 08
10 9 8 7 6 5 4 3 2 1

Library of Congress Cataloging-in-Publication Data
Harris, Nancy, 1956-
  What's the Declaration of Independence? / Nancy Harris.
    p. cm. -- (First guide to government)
  Includes bibliographical references and index.
  ISBN 978-1-4329-0984-0 (hc) -- ISBN 978-1-4329-0990-1 (pb) 1. United States. Declaration of Independence--Juvenile literature. 2. United States--Politics and government--1775-1783--Juvenile literature.
I. Title.
  E221.H23 2008
  973.3'13--dc22
                          2008001154

Acknowledgments
The author and publisher are grateful to the following for permission to reproduce copyright material: ©Corbis **p. 29** (Kevin Dodge); ©Getty Images **p. 16** (Stock Montage); ©North Wind Picture Archives **pp. 6** (North Wind), **18** (North Wind); ©Redux **p. 28** (The New York Times/Paul Hosefros); ©The Bridgeman Art Library International **pp. 13** (Atwater Kent Museum of Philadelphia, Courtesy of Historical Society of Pennsylvania Collection), **24** (Boltin Picture Library), **25** (Private Collection, Peter Newark American Pictures); ©The Granger Collection, New York, **pp. 7, 8, 9, 10, 11, 12, 14, 15, 17, 19, 21, 26, 27**; ©The National Archives and Records Administration **pp. 5, 20, 22, 23**.

Cover image used with permission of ©The Bridgeman Art Library International (Private Collection, Peter Newark American Pictures).

The publishers would like to thank Nancy Harris for her assistance in the preparation of this book.

Every effort has been made to contact copyright holders of any material reproduced in this book. Any omissions will be rectified in subsequent printings if notice is given to the publisher.

Disclaimer
All the Internet addresses (URLs) given in this book were valid at the time of going to press. However, due to the dynamic nature of the Internet, some addresses may have changed, or sites may have changed or ceased to exist since publication. While the author and publisher regret any inconvenience this may cause readers, no responsibility for any such changes can be accepted by either the author or the publisher.

Contents

Some words are shown in bold, **like this**. You can find out what they mean by looking in the glossary.

What Is the Declaration of Independence?

The Declaration of Independence is a very important **document** (paper). It was written by a group of men who lived in the American **colonies**. The colonies were ruled by Great Britain. The colonies later became the United States of America.

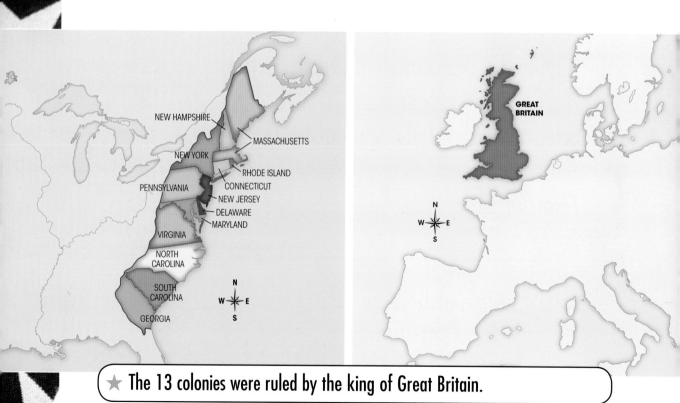

★ The 13 colonies were ruled by the king of Great Britain.

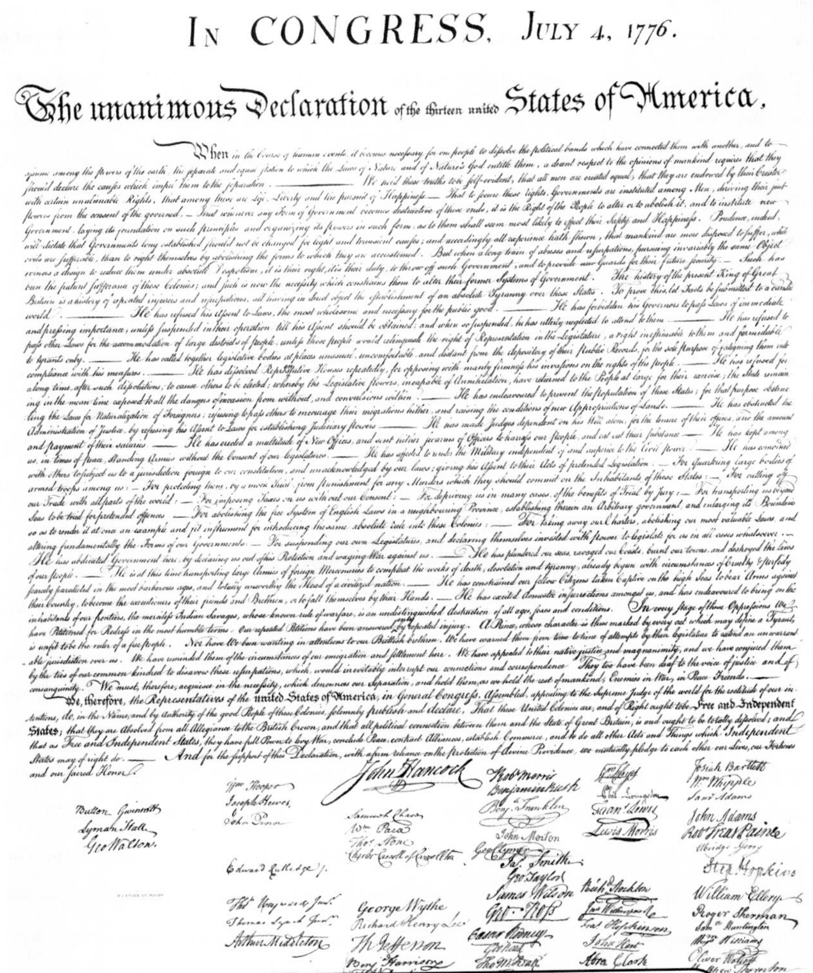

IN CONGRESS, JULY 4, 1776.

The unanimous Declaration of the thirteen united States of America,

When in the Course of human events, it becomes necessary for one people to dissolve the political bands which have connected them with another, and to assume among the powers of the earth, the separate and equal station to which the Laws of Nature and of Nature's God entitle them, a decent respect to the opinions of mankind requires that they should declare the causes which impel them to the separation. — We hold these truths to be self-evident, that all men are created equal, that they are endowed by their Creator with certain unalienable Rights, that among these are Life, Liberty and the pursuit of Happiness. — That to secure these rights, Governments are instituted among Men, deriving their just powers from the consent of the governed, — That whenever any Form of Government becomes destructive of these ends, it is the Right of the People to alter or to abolish it, and to institute new Government, laying its foundation on such principles and organizing its powers in such form, as to them shall seem most likely to effect their Safety and Happiness. Prudence, indeed, will dictate that Governments long established should not be changed for light and transient causes; and accordingly all experience hath shewn, that mankind are more disposed to suffer, while evils are sufferable, than to right themselves by abolishing the forms to which they are accustomed. But when a long train of abuses and usurpations, pursuing invariably the same Object evinces a design to reduce them under absolute Despotism, it is their right, it is their duty, to throw off such Government, and to provide new Guards for their future security. — Such has been the patient sufferance of these Colonies; and such is now the necessity which constrains them to alter their former Systems of Government. The history of the present King of Great Britain is a history of repeated injuries and usurpations, all having in direct object the establishment of an absolute Tyranny over these States. To prove this, let Facts be submitted to a candid world.

★ The Declaration of Independence was a letter to the king of Great Britain.

The Declaration of Independence was written to the king of Great Britain. The document said that the American colonies were breaking away from Great Britain. The people in the colonies no longer wanted to be ruled by the king. They wanted to form a new country.

The American Colonies

There were 13 **colonies** in North America. A colony is a place people move to from another country. The people who live there are called **colonists**. Colonists are ruled by the leader of the country they came from.

★ The colonists did not like being ruled by Great Britain.

The people in the 13 colonies were ruled by the king of Great Britain. His name was King George the Third. The king made **laws** (rules) the colonists had to obey.

★ King George the Third was very powerful.

Unhappy Colonists

The **colonists** did not like being ruled by the king of Great Britain. They felt they were being treated unfairly by the king.

★ Colonists lit fires to show their anger with the king.

★ The king sent letters to the colonies about new laws.

The king made **laws** the colonists did not like. They felt the laws were wrong. They felt that the laws were hurting the colonists.

Taxes

The king made the **colonists** pay money to Great Britain. This money was called a **tax**. The king made the colonists pay taxes for tea and paper. The colonists felt the taxes were too high.

★ Colonists fought against the tax on tea.

★ Colonists were angry when the king taxed paper for stamps.

The colonists felt they should be able to help decide how they were ruled. They felt they should help decide what taxes they should pay. They wanted the king to listen to their thoughts and needs.

Taking a Stand

King George the Third did not listen to what the **colonists** wanted. He continued to rule them from a distance. This made the colonists very unhappy.

Colonists in New York pulled the king's statue down to show their anger.

The colonists wanted to decide how they were led.
A group of men met in the city of Philadelphia.
They met to decide what to do next.

★ The colonists met in Carpenter's Hall in Philadelphia.

The Second Continental Congress

★★★ The Second Continental Congress was led by George Washington.

The men met at the State House in Philadelphia. They belonged to a group called the **Second Continental Congress**. The members of the group included one man from each of the 13 **colonies** except for Georgia.

The group decided they needed to separate from Great Britain. They chose a **committee** (group) to write a paper to King George the Third. The paper would say why the **colonists** were separating from Great Britain.

★ The group worked together to write their ideas to the king.

Writing the Declaration of Independence

A **committee** of five men was formed to write the paper. One member was asked to write the first draft. This man was Thomas Jefferson.

★★★ Thomas Jefferson later became the third president of the United States.

★★★ Thomas Jefferson worked to make sure that the document said what the colonists wanted.

Thomas Jefferson was very careful in writing the **document**. He wrote it to represent the feelings of the **colonists**. He wanted King George the Third to understand how they felt.

Thomas Jefferson knew that the United States might need help from leaders of other countries.

He also wrote it to get support from other countries. The **colonies** were about to become a new country. He knew they may need help from other countries.

★ These men added changes to the first draft.

After Jefferson finished his draft, it was read by the other four committee members. The four members were John Adams, Benjamin Franklin, Roger Sherman, and Robert Livingston. They made changes to the **document**.

The Declaration of Independence

Preamble

The first part of the Declaration of Independence is the **preamble**. It explains why the Declaration of Independence was written. It explains why the **colonists** were breaking away from Great Britain. It says why they wanted to be **independent** (free) from British rule.

In CONGRESS, July 4, 1776.

The unanimous Declaration of the thirteen united States of America.

★ The Preamble tells the king that everyone deserves life, liberty and the pursuit of happiness.

The authors thought carefully about the rights of the colonists.

Government and Rights

The authors of the Declaration of Independence say how a **government** should work. They talk about the **rights** of the colonists. Rights are freedoms that people have. The authors wrote that people had the right to help decide how they were led.

King George the Third

Next, the authors include a list of how King George the Third had been unfair to the **colonists**. They wanted people in other countries to understand why the colonists were separating from British rule.

★ The colonists had many complaints about the king.

Independence

At the end of the document, the authors say that the **colonies** are now separated from Great Britain. They are **independent** from British rule. The colonies are now states that may decide how to lead themselves.

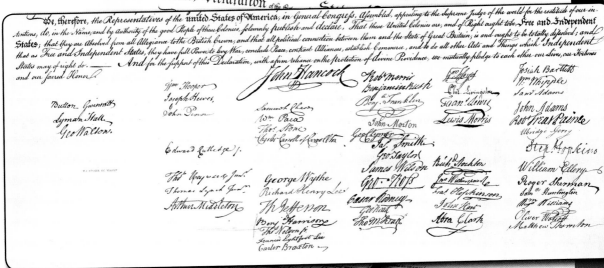

★★★ The end of the Declaration of Independence made the colonies free.

Signing the Declaration of Independence

★★★★ It was important to make sure everyone agreed on the Declaration of Independence.

The final **document** was read by all the members of the **Second Continental Congress**. The group voted in favor of the document on July 4, 1776. The document was also read and **approved** by people in the 13 **colonies**.

The Declaration of Independence was signed on August 2, 1776 by the members of the Second Continental Congress. It has 56 signatures. The first person to sign it was John Hancock. John Hancock was the leader of the Second Continental Congress.

★ John Hancock's signature is the biggest.

The Revolutionary War

The **colonists** fought in a war against Great Britain. This war was fought to gain freedom from British rule. The war started in 1775. It was called the Revolutionary War.

★ The colonists had to fight for their freedom.

★ The colonists celebrated after the war.

The Declaration of Independence was written during the war. The colonists won the war in 1783. They became independent from British rule and formed the United States of America.

Celebrating the Declaration of Independence

★★★ President George W. Bush and First Lady Laura Bush look at the Declaration of Independence.

The Declaration of Independence is now on display in the National Archives building. Visitors can look at the **document** during visiting hours. The National Archives is located in Washington, D.C., our nation's capital.

★ The Declaration of Independence gave Americans freedom!

The Declaration of Independence was the beginning of a new country. The new country is called the United States of America. Every year on the Fourth of July, people in the United States celebrate their independence.

Glossary

approve agree with something

colony place people move to from another country. A colony is ruled by the country the people moved from.

colonist person who lives in a colony

committee group of people who are chosen to do a specific job

document written text or paper. The Declaration of Independence is a document.

independent when you are free to decide how you live and what you do

government group of leaders who make laws for a city, state, or country

law rule people must obey in a state or country

preamble first part of a text. It is written to tell why the paper was written.

rights freedoms that people have. Rights include the right to say and write what you think.

Second Continental Congress group of people that included a man from each of the 13 colonies. They met to represent the needs of the people in their colony.

tax money that a person has to pay to a state or country

trade buy or sell goods to another person, state, or country. This could include selling food, clothes, and other goods.

Find Out More

Books to Read

Furgang, Kathy. *The Declaration of Independence and Thomas Jefferson of Virginia.* New York: Rosen Publishing, 2002.

Rosen, Daniel. *Independence Now: The American Revolution, 1763-1783.* Washington, DC: National Geographic, 2004.

Yero, Judith Lloyd. *The Declaration of Independence.* Washington, DC: National Geographic, 2006.

Websites

Ben's Guide to U.S. Government
Visit **http://bensguide.gpo.gov/** to play games and learn the ABCs of the United States Government.

Viewing the Declaration of Independence

The Declaration of Independence is on display in the National Archives in the Rotunda. The Rotunda is open daily from 9 am to 5pm during fall and winter and from 10 am to 7 pm during spring and summer.

The National Archives address is:
700 Pennsylvania Avenue, NW
Washington, DC 20408

Index